New Jersey

Jill Wheeler

Visit us at
www.abdopublishing.com

Editor: John Hamilton
Graphic Design: Sue Hamilton
Cover Illustration: Neil Klinepier
Cover Photo: iStock Photo
Interior Photo Credits: AirPhoto/Jim Wark, Alamy, AP Images, Comstock, Corbis, David Listemaa, Getty, Granger Collection, Gunter Küchler, iStock Photo, Kesha Linehan, Library of Congress, Mile High Maps, Mountain High Maps, New Jersey Devils, New Jersey Nets, New York Giants, New York Jets, and One Mile Up.
Statistics: State population statistics taken from 2008 U.S. Census Bureau estimates. City and town population statistics taken from July 1, 2007, U.S. Census Bureau estimates. Land and water area statistics taken from 2000 Census, U.S. Census Bureau.

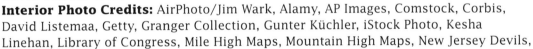

Manufactured with paper containing at least 10% post-consumer waste

Library of Congress Cataloging-in-Publication Data

Wheeler, Jill C., 1964-
  New Jersey / Jill C. Wheeler.
       p. cm. -- (The United States)
  Includes index.
  ISBN 978-1-60453-665-2
  1. New Jersey--Juvenile literature. I. Title.

F134.3.W53 2010
974.9--dc22
                                    2008051721

3 1561 00230 1814

Table of Contents

The Garden State 4

Quick Facts 6

Geography 8

Climate and Weather 12

Plants and Animals 14

History 18

Did You Know? 24

People 26

Cities 30

Transportation 34

Natural Resources 36

Industry 38

Sports 40

Entertainment 42

Timeline 44

Glossary 46

Index 48

The Garden State

New Jersey is a state rich in history and resources. It was the third state to join the United States. It is the fourth-smallest state. People call New Jersey the Garden State because it has so much farmland. In fact, farmland covers one-eighth of the state. New Jersey is the largest commercial fruit and vegetable canning state in the country.

New Jersey is home to beautiful forests, plus many other natural features. Many people who work in New York City and Philadelphia, Pennsylvania, choose to live in New Jersey. They like the beauty of New Jersey so much they are willing to commute long distances each day.

Canoeists paddle on the Batsto River in the beautiful Pine Barrens region of New Jersey.

Quick Facts

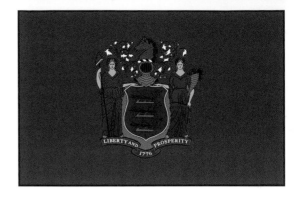

Name: New Jersey is named after England's Isle of Jersey by the Duke of York.

State Capital: Trenton, population 82,804

Date of Statehood: December 18, 1787 (3rd state)

Population: 8,682,661 (11th-most populous state)

Area (Total Land and Water): 8,721 square miles (22,587 sq km), 47th-largest state

Largest City: Newark, population 280,135

Nickname: The Garden State

Motto: Liberty and Prosperity

State Bird: Eastern Goldfinch

State Flower: Common Violet

State Tree: Red Oak

Highest Point: 1,803 feet (550 m), High Point

Lowest Point: 0 feet (0 m) Atlantic Ocean

Average July Temperature: 73°F (23°C)

Record High Temperature: 110°F (43°C) at Runyon, July 10, 1936

Average January Temperature: 30°F (-1°C)

Record Low Temperature: -34°F (-37°C) at River Vale, January 5, 1904

Average Annual Precipitation: 45 inches (114 cm)

Number of U.S. Senators: 2

Number of U.S. Representatives: 13

U.S. Presidents Born in New Jersey: Grover Cleveland (1837-1908)

U.S. Postal Service Abbreviation: NJ

High Point

Grover Cleveland

Geography

New Jersey is the fourth-smallest state. Even so, it has many different terrains. If you drive through New Jersey, you will see pine forests, marshes, meadows, beaches, rolling hills, and flowing rivers. The Appalachian Mountains and the Appalachian Valley are located on the state's northwestern edge. Many cows graze in this area. Apple orchards fill the valleys.

The Kittatinny Mountains are found in the Appalachian Mountains. High Point is located within this long ridge of mountains. High Point is New Jersey's highest spot. It is 1,803 feet (550 m) high.

The Highlands are east of the Appalachian Valley. They are known for their rocky terrain and many lakes.

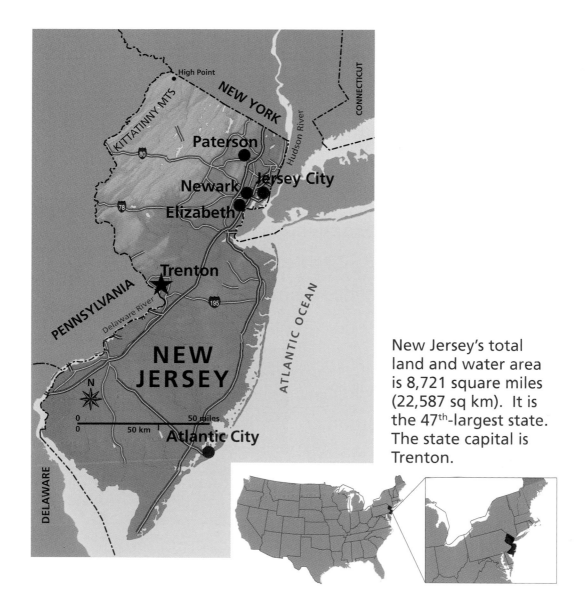

New Jersey's total land and water area is 8,721 square miles (22,587 sq km). It is the 47th-largest state. The state capital is Trenton.

The Piedmont region is in the northeast corner of the state. The Hudson and Delaware Rivers flow through the Piedmont. Many large, industrial cities are here.

In the southern three-fifths of New Jersey, farms, forests, marshes, and beaches make up the Atlantic Coastal Plain.

The New Jersey Palisades are in the Piedmont. They stretch for 20 miles (32 km) and range from 350 to 550 feet (107 to 168 m) tall.

The Delaware Water Gap is a geographical landmark found in the Piedmont. The Delaware River has carved out a beautiful gorge in this area.

A hiker looks down at the Delaware Water Gap.

The Great Falls is a very big waterfall located in the Passaic River. It is 77 feet (23 m) high. It was very important to early industry in New Jersey. Many visitors to New Jersey make a point to see these beautiful natural landmarks.

The Great Falls on the Passaic River.

Climate and Weather

People enjoy New Jersey's sun and sand.

The weather in New Jersey is moderate. This means the state rarely gets very cold or very hot. The average July temperature is 73 degrees Fahrenheit (23°C). The average January temperature is 30 degrees Fahrenheit (-1°C).

Northwest New Jersey has fairly harsh winters. It is often cold and snowy there. River Vale in northern New Jersey had the lowest recorded temperature in the state. It was -34 degrees Fahrenheit (-37°C) in River Vale on January 5, 1904.

The rest of New Jersey has milder winters. In the south, it is rarely very cold.

Wind-driven waves crash along the shoreline in Avalon, New Jersey. The state received tropical storm force winds from Hurricane Isabel in 2003.

Sometimes large tropical storms hit New Jersey in the summer. These storms can cause flooding and strong winds. Tropical storms may turn into hurricanes, but this does not often happen in New Jersey. New Jersey has an average of 45 inches (114 cm) of precipitation each year.

Plants and Animals

There are approximately 500 species of animals in New Jersey. Wild turkeys, deer, and bears are all found in New Jersey. Red and grey foxes, muskrats, coyotes, otters, raccoons, skunks, opossums, and rabbits also call New Jersey home. Many animals live in New Jersey's rivers, lakes, and ocean shore, too. These include bullfrogs, green frogs, and snapping turtles.

Freshwater fish include largemouth bass, pickerels,

Bluefish

and catfish. Saltwater fish in New Jersey include bluefish, flounder, mackerel, and striped bass.

The state also is home to approximately 300 bird species. The state bird is the eastern goldfinch.

A bear peers from a tree in Parsippany, New Jersey.

Snowy Owl

Turtles

Goldfinch

The Pine Barrens treefrog is endangered.

About one-fourth of southern New Jersey is covered by an amazing forest. The Pinelands Forest is also known as the Pine Barrens. It is home to about 150 species of animals. More than 40 of these animals are endangered or threatened. The Pine Barrens treefrog is one of these endangered species.

New Jersey's state tree is the red oak, which can be found throughout the state. Buttercups, daisies, Queen Anne's lace, purple violets, lady's slippers, skunk cabbage, and jack-in-the-pulpit all can be seen in New Jersey. There are also azalea and rhododendron bushes.

Azalea   Purple Violet   Lady's Slipper   Jack-in-the-Pulpit

History

The first people who came to the New Jersey area arrived about 10,000 years ago. These Native Americans were called the Delaware Indians. They were also called the Lenni Lenape, which means "original people." They lived in eastern Canada, parts of New York,

A New Jersey Native American drawing.

Pennsylvania, Delaware, and all across New Jersey.

There were three groups of Lenni Lenape. Each had its own symbol. The Munsee used a wolf as a symbol. They lived in northern New Jersey. The Unami's symbol was a turtle. The Unami lived in the center of the state. The Unalachtigo chose a turkey as their symbol. They lived in southern New Jersey.

The first Europeans to visit the area came in 1524. At that time, Italian explorer Giovanni da Verrazzano anchored off the New Jersey shore. He saw the shore but did not leave his ship. The next European visitors came 85 years later. In 1609, English explorer Henry Hudson sailed up the Hudson River. He claimed all of the land around the river for his employer, the Dutch government. This included much of today's New Jersey. The Dutch called the land New Netherlands.

In 1664, the Dutch lost control of New Netherlands to the British. The British added the land to their American colonies and named it New Jersey. It was named after the Isle of Jersey, in the English Channel.

In 1665, Englishman Philip Carteret was appointed leader of New Jersey after the English gained control of the area.

The early colony of New Jersey had very harsh laws. People were punished for saying bad words or drinking too much alcohol. However, people from New Jersey did not always follow the laws. In 1774, citizens got very frustrated by unfair British taxes on tea. They stole a large shipment of the tea and burned it in a field.

New Jersey was divided during the Revolutionary War. Many people wanted independence from England, but others supported England. They were called Tories.

New Jersey lies between New York and Pennsylvania. This made it very important during the Revolutionary War. Armies often crossed New Jersey, or fought battles there. The Battle of Trenton and the Battle of Princeton were both fought in New Jersey. New Jersey became known as the Crossroads of the Revolution.

George Washington led a surprise attack at Trenton, New Jersey.

In 1787, New Jersey became the third state to ratify, or approve, the United States Constitution. Trenton became the official state capital in 1790. The state's first governor was William Livingston.

New Jersey was mainly rural for much of the 1800s. Cities and factories eventually sprang up. Textiles, clay, and iron were important products produced in the state. Many immigrants came to work in New Jersey's factories.

William Livingston was the first governor of New Jersey.

During the Civil War (1861-1865), New Jersey was on the side of the North against the Confederate South. More than 25,000 New Jersey soldiers fought for the Union.

Thomas Edison was known as the New Jersey Wizard of Electricity.

New Jersey's governor, Woodrow Wilson, became the 28th president.

New Jersey continued to build factories after the Civil War. Inventors like Thomas Edison helped the state's industry grow. In 1913, New Jersey Governor Woodrow Wilson became president of the United States.

The Great Depression of the 1930s hit New Jersey hard. Factories were forced to close. Many people lost jobs.

During World War II and the 1940s, New Jersey's economy started to bounce back. The government also put many people back to work building new roads, bridges, and airports.

During the 1960s and early 1970s, people in some New Jersey cities fought over equal rights. They protested poverty, unemployment, and poor housing for African Americans. The state began economic projects and city reforms that would help people of all races. Some New Jersey cities still struggle with poverty and poor education.

In the 1970s, and again in the early 1990s, many factories shut down or left the state. New Jersey started to diversify its economy. It expanded into services, such as tourism. Today, the state is better able to weather economic hardships.

Did You Know?

Samuel F.B. Morse

Alfred Vail

- The world's first telegraph was sent from an iron mill in Morristown, New Jersey, on January 6, 1838. Samuel F.B. Morse sent a message to Alfred Vail, his assistant. The message was in a code of dots and dashes now called Morse code. It read, "A patient waiter is no loser."

- Some New Jersey towns are called "bedroom communities" because so many people live in New Jersey but work in New York City or Philadelphia, Pennsylvania.

- Even though New Jersey is the fourth-smallest state, it is home to many people.

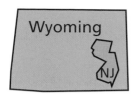

Wyoming

NJ

In comparison, Wyoming is the 10th-largest state. Yet, New Jersey has more than 16 times the population of Wyoming.

- One of the country's busiest suspension bridges is in New Jersey. The George Washington Bridge has 2 levels and 14 lanes. It is supported by four cables, each made of 26,474 individual wires.

You frowning at me?

- Like many states, New Jersey has some strange laws. For example, cabbage can't be sold on Sundays. It is against the law for a man to knit during fishing season. In Newark, it is illegal to sell ice cream after 6:00 pm unless the customer has a note from a doctor. Finally, it is against the law to frown at a police officer.

DID YOU KNOW?

People

Grover Cleveland (1837-1908) was born in Caldwell, New Jersey. He was the only president to serve two non-consecutive terms. He was president from 1885 to 1889, and from 1893 to 1897. He also is the only president born in New Jersey.

Aaron Burr (1756-1836) was vice president of the United States from 1801 to 1805. He served under President Thomas Jefferson. In 1804, he had a fight with political rival Alexander Hamilton. Hamilton was killed in the pistol duel. Aaron Burr was born in Newark.

Walt Whitman (1819-1892) was one of America's greatest poets. He lived in Camden, New Jersey, for 19 years. His most famous poems were put into a book called *Leaves of Grass*.

Lawrence Peter "Yogi" Berra (1925-) was a Major League Baseball catcher from 1946 to 1965. He played most of his career for the New York Yankees. He was given the American League's Most Valuable Player Award three times. He also managed both the Yankees and the New York Mets. He and his family have lived in Montclair, New Jersey, for many years.

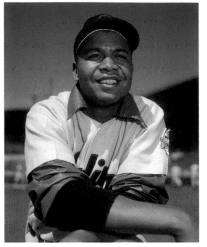

Larry Doby (1923-2003) was the second African American player in Major League Baseball. He grew up in Paterson, New Jersey. Before joining the Cleveland Indians in 1947, he played for the Newark Eagles in the Negro League.

Kirsten Dunst (1982-) is a famous actress. She has starred in many movies. She is most well known as Mary Jane Watson, Spider-Man's girlfriend, in the *Spider-Man* movies. She was born in Point Pleasant, New Jersey.

Queen Latifah (1970-) was born in Newark, New Jersey. Her real name is Dana Owens. This famous female rap singer has also been in several popular movies. She has won many awards for her work in music and film.

Bruce Springsteen (1949-) is a popular singer, songwriter, and musician. He was born in Long Branch in 1949, but he grew up in Freehold. Bruce Springsteen started singing in nightclubs on the boardwalk in Asbury Park. His most famous album is 1984's *Born in the U.S.A.*

Cities

Trenton originally was settled by the Quakers. The city was named

Trenton became New Jersey's capital in 1790.

after William Trent. He was a merchant who helped develop the area in the early 1700s. Trenton became New Jersey's capital city in 1790. About 82,804 people live in Trenton. Visitors can see the state capitol building, the Washington Crossing State Park where General George Washington crossed the Delaware River, and the New Jersey State Museum. The State Museum features Native American artifacts, a mastodon skeleton, and a replica of a mine.

Newark is New Jersey's largest city. It has a population of about 280,135. Newark is the center of the state's performing arts community. The New Jersey Symphony Orchestra, New Jersey State Opera, and many theaters and dance companies call Newark home.

Newark's nickname is the Brick City, because of all the brick buildings.

Jersey City has a population of about 242,389. It is close to New York City. From Jersey City, visitors can travel to Liberty State Park or take the ferry to the Statue of Liberty and Ellis Island. Jersey City also is home to the Liberty Science Center. The center features exhibits on everything from earthquakes to how the human body works.

The city of **Paterson** has about 146,545 residents. It was named after William Paterson. He was the governor of New Jersey from 1790 to 1793. Paterson is known as the Silk City because its factories produced so much silk and other fabrics in the late 1800s.

Atlantic City is famous for its casinos. The city's first casino opened in 1978. There are many other attractions as well. Atlantic City has a world-famous boardwalk, where visitors can buy popular snacks such as saltwater taffy. In addition, visitors to Gardner's Basin, a waterfront park, can watch dolphins and whales. Atlantic City has a population of about 39,684.

The city of **Elizabeth** is home to about 124,862 people. Its train stations, highways, and marinas have made the city an important East Coast transportation hub. It has a diverse population representing more than 50 countries.

Transportation

The New Jersey Turnpike, built from 1950 to 1952, is one of the busiest highways in the country.

For many years, New Jersey has been a crossroads of the East Coast. Many people travel through the state on their way to big cities like New York or Philadelphia, Pennsylvania. The most famous highway in the state is the New Jersey Turnpike. It carries traffic between Delaware and New York.

The Garden State Parkway is another important highway. It connects New York City with Atlantic City. Many train and bus routes also crisscross the state.

George Washington Bridge

The George Washington Bridge crosses the Hudson River. It is the world's only 14-lane suspension bridge. Built in 1931, the bridge has two decks.

Newark Liberty International Airport is one of the country's busiest airports. Several other airports also serve New Jersey.

People in New Jersey have long used lakes, rivers, and the ocean to get goods from place to place. Today, there are many ferryboats that take people to work in neighboring states.

Natural Resources

About one-eighth of the land in New Jersey is farmland. There are approximately 10,327 farms. Decorative flowers are a very profitable farm product in New Jersey. Farmers in the state also grow apples, asparagus, peaches, peppers, cauliflower, cabbage, cranberries, blueberries,

A New Jersey pick-your-own blueberry farm.

eggplants, spinach and snap peas. The state is a top producer of crops in the United States. It also is famous for commercially canned fruits and vegetables.

Fishing and mining are popular in New Jersey, too. The most common seafood items in New Jersey are clams, smelt, bluefish, porgies, striped bass, swordfish, squid, and flounder.

Several minerals are mined in New Jersey, including sand, gravel, and granite. Peat and greensand marl also are mined in central New Jersey. These are used as fertilizers.

Many minerals are mined in New Jersey, including sand, gravel, and granite.

Industry

More than five million people work in New Jersey. Many of them work in service industries. These include teachers, doctors, government officials, salespeople, and restaurant workers. The service industries that employ the most people are banks and insurance companies. Tourism also is a growing service industry.

Manufacturing is New Jersey's second-largest industry. About eight percent of the people living in New Jersey work in manufacturing. New Jersey is the nation's top producer of chemicals, including soap, cosmetics, and medicines. Machinery, clothing, electronics, metal products, and many snack foods also are produced in New Jersey.

People walk through the M&M factory in Hackettstown, New Jersey. The plant runs 24-hours a day, every day. An amazing 100 million M&Ms are made every eight hours.

The M&M factory is in Hackettstown. Oreos are made in Fair Lawn, as well as other Nabisco snacks.

Many other companies also call New Jersey home. These include the drug companies of Johnson & Johnson, Merck, and Hoffman-La Roche. Dozens of communications companies, such as Tyco International, also have headquarters in New Jersey.

Sports

Two professional football teams play in New Jersey, the Jets and the Giants. Both of these teams play in New Jersey, but are considered New York teams. New Jersey does have its own basketball team, the Nets. The state also has its own hockey team, the Devils. Horse racing is a popular sport in New Jersey as well. In addition, the U.S. Equestrian Team trains in the Garden State.

In 1976, the Meadowlands Sports Complex opened in East Rutherford. Since then, the Women's and Men's Soccer World Cup semifinals have been held there.

Outdoor enthusiasts find many activities in New Jersey. There are many beaches along the coast. Also, lakeside resorts offer boating, water skiing, and swimming. Hiking, canoeing, and picnicking are popular in the Delaware Water Gap. Mountain Creek, one of the East Coast's largest ski resorts, offers excellent skiing opportunities.

In 2005, competitors performed in the Chevrolet US Snowboard Grand Prix at the popular Mountain Creek Resort in Vernon, New Jersey.

Entertainment

There are many things to do in New Jersey. In Margate City, visitors can go inside Lucy, a 129-year-old, 65-foot (20-m) high wooden elephant. In Trenton, history buffs can watch a re-enactment of General George Washington crossing the Delaware River. At the Old Barracks

Now a National Historic Landmark, Lucy was once used as a restaurant, a business office, a hotel, and a bar.

Museum, visitors can see where Washington's army ate and slept. They can also learn how surgeons and doctors worked during the Revolutionary War.

Glass-blown items are sold at a store in Wheaton Village.

In Rancocas, the American Indian Heritage Museum focuses on the Lenni Lenape people. In Wheaton Village, there is a glass-blowing factory that is open for tours.

Newark is home to many performing arts events and festivals, including orchestra, opera, theater, and dance. Newark also is known for its St. Patrick's Day Parade, where many different cultures and nationalities are on display.

Timeline

1524—Explorer Giovanni da Verrazzano is the first European to see present-day New Jersey.

1609—Explorer Henry Hudson sails up the Hudson River and claims the New Jersey area for the Dutch.

1660—The town of Bergen is established. It becomes New Jersey's first town. Today it is called Jersey City.

1664—All of New Jersey and some of the surrounding area are given to the Duke of York.

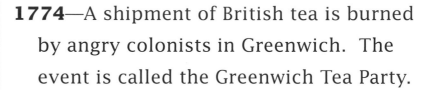

1774—A shipment of British tea is burned by angry colonists in Greenwich. The event is called the Greenwich Tea Party.

1787—New Jersey becomes the third state.

1876—Thomas Edison opens a research and development lab in Menlo Park.

1931—The George Washington Bridge, the world's only 14-lane bridge, opens.

1976—Casino gambling for Atlantic City is legalized, revitalizing the city.

1994-2001—Christine Todd Whitman takes office as New Jersey's first woman governor.

Glossary

Commute—Travel between a person's work and home.

Equestrian—Horseback riding or horseback riders.

Gorge—A narrow cleft with steep, rocky walls, like a small canyon.

Mastodon—An extinct mammal that lived long ago. The animal looked like a large elephant. Remains of the creature have been found all around the world.

Moderate—Not severe, or harsh.

Morse Code—A system of dots and dashes used to represent the letters of the alphabet in a telegraph.

Negro—A person with dark skin. Today, they are usually called African Americans, or blacks.

Non-Consecutive—Not one after the other.

NEW JERSEY

Quaker—A member of the Religious Society of Friends. Quakers are a Christian group that was founded in 1650 by George Fox.

Species—A class of plants or animals that are very similar.

Suspension Bridge—A bridge with its deck supported by large cables hung from towers.

Telegraph—A machine that sends electronic signals representing letters of the alphabet and numbers across great distances along a wire. The message is also known as a telegraph.

Tories—People loyal to England during the American Revolutionary War (1775-1783).

Tropical Storm—A storm with winds between 39 and 73 mph (63 and 117 kph). Tropical storms can create significant rainfall. Their winds can cause beach erosion and damage coastal structures. Tropical storms sometimes strengthen to become hurricanes.

Index

A

American Indian Heritage
  Museum 43
American League 27
Appalachian Mountains 8
Appalachian Valley 8
Asbury Park, NJ 29
Atlantic City, NJ 33, 35
Atlantic Coastal Plain 10

B

Berra, Lawrence Peter
  "Yogi" 27
Boardwalk 33
Born in the U.S.A. 29
Burr, Aaron 26

C

Caldwell, NJ 26
Camden, NJ 27
Canada 18
Civil War 21, 22
Cleveland, Grover 26
Cleveland Indians 28
Confederates 21
Constitution, US 21

D

Delaware 18, 34
Delaware (tribe) 18
Delaware River 10, 30, 42
Delaware Water Gap 10,
  41
Doby, Larry 28
Dunst, Kirsten 28

E

East Coast 33, 34, 41
East Rutherford, NJ 40
Edison, Thomas 22
Elizabeth, NJ 33
Ellis Island 32
England 20
English Channel 19
Equestrian Team, U.S. 40

F

Fair Lawn, NJ 39
Freehold, NJ 29

G

Garden State Parkway 35
Gardner's Basin 33
George Washington Bridge
  25, 35
Great Depression 22
Great Falls 11

H

Hackettstown, NJ 39
Hamilton, Alexander 26
High Point 8
Highlands 8
Hoffman-La Roche 39
Hudson, Henry 19
Hudson River 10, 19, 35

I

Isle of Jersey 19

J

Jefferson, Thomas 26
Jersey City, NJ 32
Johnson & Johnson 39

K

Kittatinny Mountains 8

L

Latifah, Queen 29
Leaves of Grass 27
Lenni Lenape (tribe) 18,
  43
Liberty Science Center 32
Liberty State Park 32
Livingston, William 21
Long Branch, NJ 29
Lucy 42

M

Major League Baseball
  27, 28
Margate City, NJ 42
Meadowlands Sports
  Complex 40
Merck 39
M&M factory 39

Montclair, NJ 27
Morristown, NJ 24
Morse, Samuel F.B. 24
Morse code 24
Mountain Creek 41
Munsee (tribe) 18

N

Nabisco 39
Negro League 28
New Jersey Devils 40
New Jersey State Museum
  30
New Jersey State Opera
  31
New Jersey Symphony
  Orchestra 31
New Jersey Turnpike 34
New Netherlands 19
New York 18, 20, 34
New York City, NY 4, 24,
  32, 34, 35
New York Giants 40
New York Jets 40
New York Mets 27
New York Yankees 27
Newark, NJ 25, 26, 29,
  31, 43
Newark Eagles 28
Newark Liberty
  International Airport
  35

O

Old Barracks Museum 42
Oreos 39
Owens, Dana 29

P

Palisades 10
Passaic River 11
Paterson, NJ 28, 32
Paterson, William 32
Pennsylvania 4, 18, 20,
  24, 34
Philadelphia, PA 4, 24, 34
Piedmont region 10
Pine Barrens 16
Pinelands Forest 16
Point Pleasant, NJ 28
Princeton, Battle of 20

Q

Quakers 30

R

Rancocas, NJ 43
Revolutionary War 20, 42
River Vale, NJ 12

S

Spider-Man 28
Spider-Man (movie) 28
Springsteen, Bruce 29
St. Patrick's Day Parade 43
Statue of Liberty 32

T

Tories 20
Trent, William 30
Trenton, NJ 21, 30, 42
Trenton, Battle of 20
Tyco International 39

U

Unalachtigo (tribe) 18
Unami (tribe) 18
Union 21
United States 4, 21, 22,
  25, 26, 36

V

Vail, Alfred 24
Verrazzano, Giovanni da
  19

W

Washington, George 30, 42
Washington Crossing State
  Park 30
Watson, Mary Jane 28
Wheaton Village 43
Whitman, Walt 27
Wilson, Woodrow 22
World Cup 40
World War II 23
Wyoming 25